THE
NOISE
WITHIN

Tinnitus

The Gateway to Mental Health Stability

DR. JULIANNE MULLEN

Copyright © 2021 Dr. Julianne Mullen

All rights reserved. No part of this book may be reproduced or transmitted in any form or by any means, electronic, mechanical, photocopying, recording, or by any information storage and retrieval system, without certified permission in writing from the copyright author, Dr. Julianne Mullen or Publisher Phoenix Dramatherapy.

ISBN: 978-9914-40-056-4

Contact

info@phoenixdramatherapy.co.uk

www.phoenixdramatherapy.co.uk

London, UK

PHOENIX
DRAMATHERAPY

Table of Contents

Acknowledgments iv

Foreword vii

Preface ix

Scene 1: "Death Feels So Alive" 1

Scene 2: "I Shouldn't Be Here" 3

Scene 3: "What Makes You Angry?" 9

Scene 4: "We Are Half in and Half Out" 14

Scene 5: "The Cloak of Shame" 17

Scene 6: "I Lied" 21

Scene 7: "I Love You the Most" 25

Scene 8: "You just shared the truth" 30

Scene 9: "I Felt Embarrassed By ... A Robin" ... 35

Reflections on The Noise Within 45

Acknowledgments

I would like to thank Mark Williams (Tinnitus Specialist & Audiologist Harley St. London) for his expertise, support, and direction within my clinical practice and also for his encouragement to write and publish this book.

I would like to thank Joshua Jerry (Enterprises) for his enthusiasm, guidance, and support in the publication of this book.

I am very grateful for the support of my Clinical Supervisor Julia Franks, whose ongoing compassionate care and counsel have been integral to my clinical practice.

Finally, I owe a debt of gratitude to all my clients who have taught me an enormous amount about tinnitus and continue to push me to be open to all experiences and to learn more. I am truly inspired by your courage and determination to overcome this very challenging condition.

PHOENIX
DRAMATHERAPY

The Noise Within

Tinnitus

A play and guidebook about the client and therapist perspective on the universal human quest to seek the relief of suffering through self-knowledge and self-empowerment

"There is no greater agony, than bearing an untold story."

Maya Angelou

Author's Note

In this book, identifying information, occupations or professions, geographical facts (cities and streets) have been changed. Universal themes related to the psychological impact of tinnitus, namely, anxiety, suicidal ideation, self-limiting belief systems, traumatic experiences, and the nature of the therapeutic process come from my own experience. These common themes in my practice have been translated into fictional characters and stories.

The Noise Within provides a snapshot of the experience of client and therapist concerning the treatment of very bothersome tinnitus. However, the themes are universal and relevant to any psychological or emotional issue that is brought up in therapy. The 'noise' within can relate to any crisis, whether that be physical, emotional, or situational, that calls us to seek help and engage in personal therapy.

Foreword

The involuntary perception of sound, termed Tinnitus Aurium, is a commonly reported symptom that is experienced by at least 10% of the global population. For most people, the cause is rooted in complex maladaptive changes within the neurological portion of the hearing system and functional changes within higher elements of the neurology that would normally be responsible for gating signals of disinterest from conscious awareness. There are a probable array of genetic, emotional, and physiological factors that serve to predispose individuals to develop this symptom which, for some, can severely disrupt the quality of life.

The symptom is rarely linked to underlying active pathology that is correctable by medical or surgical means. From a patient perspective, this revelation can serve to induce a sense of being trapped with the symptom and induce catastrophic thoughts regarding the future prognosis. This in turn induces understandable anxiety which primes the neurology to process the tinnitus signal into conscious awareness more reliably. Patients can soon find themselves trapped in a cycle of phobic monitoring from which it is difficult to escape.

Fortunately, there is hope and, contrary to popular belief, the symptom can be ameliorated to the extent that it is rendered burden-free over time. This is not a life sentence. Audiological, physiotherapeutic, and psychological techniques can be applied to reduce tinnitus-related distress, provide control over the emotional response and promote sustainable unawareness.

Dr. Julianne Mullen's text relies upon real-life practice experience to provide an exploration of the complex emotional issues that underpin, sustain, and result from tinnitus. The issues espoused by the patients are immediately recognizable to any practitioner that works within this field and will surely resonate with sufferers. It is rare to experience the voices of distressed patients within tinnitus-related literature and rarer still to be privy to how the patient-therapist relationship can serve to promote meaningful rehabilitation. There is good reason for sufferers to feel that their future is not preordained to be bleak. Help can be sought, and life can improve. To start realizing this about the future will hopefully reduce the hardship in the present.

Mr. Mark Williams
Chief Audiologist & Tinnitus Specialist Harley St.
London

Preface

The Noise Within is a culmination of six years of clinical practice working with clients therapeutically suffering from acute and chronic tinnitus. Tinnitus is the medical term to describe the involuntary perception of noise localized to within the ears or the head. The sounds perceived are variable from person to person, but the shared link is that they do not originate from an external source. Everyone responds to tinnitus in their way. Most people with the condition aren't emotionally affected by it. Some, however, find that it intrudes on their everyday life. Tinnitus can have a harsh effect on the quality of life for around 1 percent of adults in the UK, causing stress, sleep problems, anxiety, and depression. It is for these very reasons that clients were initially referred to me.

As my clinical work progressed over the years, distinctive repetitive patterns began to emerge amongst my client cases. I noticed how the problem became less about the noise itself, and more about the reaction that clients exhibited to it. Initially, there was an apparent gap in understanding between the physiological and the emotional components of the condition. I learned how clients experienced relief from the condition when they understood how their emotional world and their physical body influenced each other. Their emotional world was hugely influenced by their patterns of thinking and more significantly their belief systems about health and illness, self-worth, and previous unprocessed trauma. These beliefs triggered anxiety, despair and exacerbated their tinnitus perception.

As a Dramatherapist, I employ creative techniques to allow clients to creatively explore their tinnitus from a distance to enable them to acquire insights and an alternative perspective on their condition. I incorporate Cognitive Behavioural Therapy techniques with Dramatherapy to disrupt patterns of negative thinking and self-limiting belief systems.

Often my clients have not experienced therapy before these sessions and have expressed how they would never have considered therapy before as an option, as they had not made the connection between their physiology and their emotional world. In my experience, once they have understood this connection, they feel more empowered and less controlled by their tinnitus. Clients have also claimed a reduction in their tinnitus perception and an overall more optimistic outlook on their lives. Therefore, I wanted to reach more tinnitus sufferers who were struggling to manage their tinnitus, to highlight the realistic possibility of experiencing life-changing habituation. This became the impetus for *The Noise*

Within. I felt that transmuting themes from clinical practice into a piece of theatre may serve to illuminate the common patterns, expressed by the characters, that could provide insight, support, and hope to others. I have included a guidebook that further explores and illuminates these patterns as a self-help tool for clinical practice and as encouragement for individuals experiencing distressful tinnitus to seek help and support.

Play

Characters

Therapist – Female in her 40s, Irish

Client 1 – Female 50s

Client 2 – Male 40s, ex-serviceman with the British Army (London accent)

SCENE 1: "DEATH FEELS SO ALIVE"

Therapist monologue could be to her therapist or clinical supervisor or God

Therapist: 'I'll take the Waterford crystal vase? The one with the robin embossed on it' she said. My mum hasn't gone into the nursing home yet. 'And can I also take the Kenwood mixer?' she asked... 'I'm sure there are a few used tissues under the bed you might like too,' I almost said to her......I should be more tolerant.... I should know better. It just hurts, you know. This is my home we are talking about. It's all I've ever known. The UK is still not on the 'green list' of countries. So, God knows when I'll get back and if I'll ever get to see her again. Every time my mum's sister calls my heart palpitations to start again. I was twelve days palpitation free until she called this morning. It's not her fault. I know it's how I respond. She's just reacting how any sister would under these circumstances......Why was she so bothered about the vase with the robin? My mum's ex-fiancé gave that to her......before she knew my father.......God knows what she wants with it. 'Take it all,' I said.

You know she rang, my aunt that is, the other day to say that my mum had said how I hadn't called in a few days and why was that. She can't remember what she had for breakfast let alone conversations she's had earlier in the day. 'You do know she is in stage 6 of Alzheimer's and that her short-term memory has been, therefore, slightly compromised,' I said. Her response was the dialling tone. She's just struggling to accept the inevitable………so am I.

I've had a full cardio assessment and there's nothing wrong with me. Yet when I get these palpitations, they force me to cough. I sound like I have final stage consumption. It acts as a good deterrent though. Keeps people at a distance if you know what I mean! Every cloud as they say…..When my aunt calls, it gets surprisingly worse……….

You know, both my grandparents died before the age of 42 from tuberculosis. So maybe I shouldn't be here much longer either. Maybe my palpitations are an echo of their passing. My grandfather died first abruptly and then my grandmother three years later. I reckon she died of a broken heart. God, death feels so alive for me at the moment. Perhaps that's why I'm not scared of death. Does that sound strange?

SCENE 2: "I SHOULDN'T BE HERE"

The therapist is in 'consult' with client 1

Client 1: I'm really scared of dying. Well, not the actual place we go, wherever that is. Just the journey getting there. I never used to think about dying until this bloody tinnitus started. I would never have considered taking my own life before. It's why I put the kitchen knife down as quickly as I had picked it up. (It was only a small one, one you'd cut an apple with….) I just want my life back the way it was….. Back to normal. I want to be able to sit in silence again and hear silence. I'm terrified that will never happen again……. Is this normal? Everything I read online says there's no cure for this. It gets worse, people eventually kill themselves because of it, just to be free of it, its torture!

Therapist: It's normal to feel this way at this stage because it is torturous. But, I would encourage you not to read online forums for the very reason that few write about recovering from tinnitus and life after tinnitus. Say a little bit more about what thoughts led you to pick up the kitchen knife.

Client 1: I had been trying to focus on my work all day. I was getting more and more frustrated. My husband came home early and was going on about the challenges his work is facing. They haven't made enough sales to break even his month yet and if it continues in this way then they'll have to declare bankruptcy…..it's a familiar rant I hear a lot. It never usually bothers me but for some reason, it did last Thursday. My tinnitus was completely overwhelming to the extent I said to him, 'Can you hear that?' 'Hear what?' he said. Everything just blurred I suppose, the sound from both my ears was so oppressive and I thought I was going to drown. I couldn't see straight and I know I needed to escape. I felt so trapped…..God, I can't bear the feeling of being trapped, with no escape…….. Yet I was trapped in myself. I kept walking into different rooms to try and escape the sound, but it kept following me. I go jogging a lot, running usually helps but not anymore. The tinnitus now screams blue murder every time I put my trainers on.

It had been one of those days last week and something odd happened…….it was as if the trip switch in my brain expired. One minute I was listening to my husband ranting about his job and the next minute I was being led upstairs by some surreal force with the kitchen knife. I closed the bedroom door and then…….. Sorry, I can't talk about it anymore. This is too difficult. I just want it to go away……I can't do this anymore. I can't live life like this anymore.

Therapist: Describe what's happening to you now.

Client 1: My chest hurts, not pain, just feels tense. I haven't shared this, the kitchen knife thing, with anyone until now. My husband doesn't even know.... It's so difficult to explain what this is like to others because it's invisible..... Everyone thinks I'm ok on the outside....but I am so not ok.....I want to scream from the top of my lungs....." I'm not ok......help me..."

Therapist: Why don't you?

Client 1: I feel ashamed about what I did. We were brought up Catholic, you're Irish, aren't you? And well to take your own life is/was, whatever..... Considered sacrilegious and it's just the shame that's unbearable.........

Therapist: Can you describe it?

Client 1: It seeps up through my feet and dries like concrete, and then tries to asphyxiate me.......

Therapist: Is that a familiar feeling?...... about the shame, before your perception of tinnitus?

Client 1: God, yes! My second name should be "shame." I've always felt full of shame. It makes me want to curl up so small and then disappear...... I've always felt that something was inherently wrong with me....Poor you,

you must get so fed up of hearing people constantly feel sorry about themselves. It's not like I've got cancer or anything…..I just can't bear this sound anymore. I feel like such a burden…….

Therapist: I hear a lot about the pain and discomfort that tinnitus sufferers endure. I am a therapist, remember. My job is to listen and I don't get fed up hearing people's stories. How was it to tell me what happened?

Client 1: A bit lighter. So how do I get rid of this noise in my ear? I've tried everything, pink noise, white noise, relaxing music, nature sounds….I even have two fans on every night. And I can still hear it…… What happens if I never stop hearing it? I can't bear the lack of control…….

Therapist: It's very challenging to escape something that is a part of us……. When you say that you always felt there was something wrong with you, how does that impact what you think and feel about yourself?

Client 1: Like I said I feel I shouldn't be here. I feel I don't have the right to be here. I tell myself I'm such a burden and that all I do is cause problems for other people. I can't even trust what I say, or what I do. I feel responsible for everything that goes wrong, not just in my life but in the world. God, that's so narcissistic………….. I hate that word narcissism…Have you ever seen Black Narcissus? Those creepy nuns used to terrify me as a child.

Therapist: What do you notice about your tinnitus when you have those thoughts and feelings?

Client 1: It gets so loud……... Do you think those thoughts make my tinnitus louder?

Therapist: What do you think?

Client 1: I'm not sure. I've felt those feelings and had those thoughts for as long as I can remember…….They are my normal way of thinking…….Oh God, I'm now feeling anxious…….

Therapist: It's ok just take your time……

Client 1: I remember the day I first heard my tinnitus. I was standing at my father's grave, this would have been six months ago. He's long dead. He died when I was eight. I went to visit his grave on his anniversary…..six months ago…..Anyway again like last Thursday with the knife……something forced me to go to his grave…something stronger than my thoughts….it's very strange and hard to explain. Am I abnormal? Do your other clients say this kind of stuff? You must think I'm a complete and utter mess.

Therapist: There is no right or wrong experience and what's normal?

Client 1: Ok…….so at the graveside I started getting flashbacks of his funeral. I was only eight so it's all a bit blurry. I remember I was wearing my 'Christmas clothes'….he died at Christmas…..great timing eh? On the day of the funeral, there was a lot of talk about whether or not I should be allowed to attend the graveside…..I was the youngest of four…..but I pleaded with my mother to let me go….Oh God, I can't talk about this……..

Therapist: You don't need to talk about anything

Client 1: I didn't want to be left out…… I remember the journey from the church to the graveside vividly. The hearse and the mourning car stopped outside our house for a few minutes before going onto the graveyard. It was beautiful…so poignant. I felt proud of him and happy that he was being given this gesture of respect. It's probably the most respect he was ever shown in his life……. then I remember feeling that heavy cloak of shame hang over my shoulders like I had done something wrong…….

SCENE 3: "WHAT MAKES YOU ANGRY?"

The therapist is in 'consult' with client 2

Client 2: Did I say something wrong?

Therapist: No, not at all. There's just something in my eye. Go on….you were saying how you first experienced tinnitus after you toured Northern Ireland …..

Client 2: Yeah. That's right………. you look like you are about to cry………

Therapist: …….I'm sorry that thing in my eye disturbed your train of thought. Just take a moment to collect your thoughts. It will come back to you.

Client 2: Yeah…… so eh I woke up a few days after I got back to London with this tinnitus screeching in my ear. This fucking noise! It is driving me mad. I saw a psychiatrist at the time, but I don't believe in any of that crap. He put me on anti-depressants for a few months. I'm sure it made it worse. Guess what one of the side effects was? Tinnitus! Anyway, I eventually got some proper sleep after taking them and it went away…..until three months ago…..

Therapist: What was happening in your life three months ago?

Client 2: Why does that matter? What's that got to do with my tinnitus and shutting it up?

Therapist: I can hear your frustration. In my experience, a lot of clients suffering from tinnitus have had an event or circumstance that was traumatic or at least caused a lot of emotional distress, before the onset of their tinnitus. There are a lot of people with tinnitus out there. I only see the ones who are emotionally and psychologically impacted by it. For that reason, I am curious about the circumstances in which you first experienced tinnitus.

Client 2: How many of your clients with tinnitus get better or *habitate (gets term wrong)* to it?

Therapist: It depends. People *habituate* in different ways at different stages. A salient trend in success rates that I notice is the willingness of the client to engage in their emotional world. It's not easy. It's scary facing our feelings. As I said to you at the start you are…

Client 2: yeah 'I'm the expert of me…..therapists are just as much in that seat as they are in this one!' Sorry.

Therapist: You seem quite angry, I could be wrong, and it's perfectly ok if you are, I'm just checking in with you to see what you are experiencing now at this moment. All feelings are valid.

Client 2: I'm fuming! And this noise keeps getting louder. It's screaming n my ear every morning, every night. It won't stop. I haven't slept properly in weeks. I've tried sleeping tablets, but I read that they can make your tinnitus worse too……..so I'm on the fucking edge here…….. Seriously if something isn't done soon……well …….

Therapist: Who else can you share this with?

Client 2: No one! Who wants to listen to me bang on about a fucking noise in my ear?

Therapist: Have you not told anyone?

Client 2: Nah

Therapist: It's a lot to hold by yourself when it can feel really disturbing and upsetting…. (*Gets interrupted by client's mobile ringing*)

Client 2: What?……. Nah nah I never said that. I'm not a fucking liar you know, You tell her to get her fucking facts straight before she starts roping me into her fucking dramas……Nah nah I'm not upset…..go on…..look you have done nothing wrong…..if you don't want to go for that job then don't….fuck them….you don't owe anyone fuck all. You do what's best for you….They are all the same. I don't give a shit anymore…..I didn't even shave for the interview today….just couldn't be bothered…..knew I wouldn't get it anyway…….yeah……..yeah…….exactly….they all fucking bitch about everyone…..I'm sure they do it about me too….yeah, I'm just not listening to their shit anymore…..and yeah she's the fucking worst of them…..gives it all the crocodile tears to your face and then stabs you in the back…..fuck them…..ok…….ok……but hold on……listen……listen………don't let then bully you..ya hear me….yeah…..I'm going to have my phone on all evening so you just call me whenever alright……..she said what? yeah but you've heard what the Head says about her?…….fucking idiot….(*laughs*)…..ok…..alright mate…..take it easy…..and listen…..remember what I said……I'm here if you need to call me…..Nah nah it's fine….you didn't disturb me at all……Nah nothing important….see …..yeah ….yeah (laughs)…alright take care ……yeah (*laughs*) ……bye mate…..bye ……bye ….bye. (*Hangs up*) Does *that* make you angry?

Therapist: What makes *you* angry?

Client 2: Your fucking accent….I'm so sorry. I didn't mean that.

Therapist: Say a bit more……. (*Long pause*)

Client 2: My wife says she doesn't love me anymore.

SCENE 4: "WE ARE HALF IN AND HALF OUT"

Therapist: 'So I hear you are very much in love,' said my mum last week on the phone. And you know, I wasn't sure who she was referring to…… So, I just played along and said, 'yes, I am.' She oscillates from one extreme to the other, one minute being completely batshit to the next being highly intuitive. I'd love to be able to tell her but……she's the only one who would get it, who would understand? She had her fair share of unconventional relationships……. Maybe when her short-term memory completely erodes, I'll tell her then. ……. I miss the fact that I can't tell her everything anymore. Well, I can, but you know, I don't want to worry her……. I've become so proficient at lying lately….with everyone…… that I feel I'm losing my already-tenuous thread with reality. I'm just trying to protect her from feeling anxious and fretful. She's been on anti-depressants most of her life….eleven tablets a day and that was still never enough to dull the anxiety. She's been mentally unstable for as long as I have known her. It's made me feel very sad over the years that I couldn't take that pain away from her……….But, there are a lot of positives to this…. If you are losing your memory, you've less to be upset and anxious about. No regrets, no nostalgia even, just oblivious bliss…….

I've read how dementia can be the soul's way of trying to leave the body, but the body is still holding on and that's why we behave as if we are losing our minds...because we are half in and half out. That would make sense. She's always been scared of dying, since the age of five, she told me. Her mother brought her to see a priest, to see if that would help reduce her fears. She had no recollection of the meeting, except for the ice cream her mum bought her afterward……she has always had this strange obsession with priests. I remember her always having a 'priest friend' when I was growing up. It's like they became locked in her psyche as a source of comfort or inoculation against death……

It's ironic though….she's spent most of her life being scared and anxious about death…and now that she's halfway there…she's no longer anxious about it…. I'm not surprised she was scared of dying, she was born at the start of the war. Her mum had lived through a world war and a civil war, what do you expect! The imprint of trauma gets passed down through the generations. I suppose my mum never had a chance. There were no counsellors or therapists in those days. Even the clergy didn't have the training to manage what they were faced with…….. It's hard grieving the loss of someone who is still alive. It comes in waves, grief…….. I cry so easily. It doesn't take much. But when that wave hits, I'm trapped and paralyzed by it until it subsides…..When I was walking the dog this morning, I stopped off to get a coffee at the park café, a nice quaint little place. I feel safe there. There's a beautiful painting of a café somewhere in Paris…..Anyway, the woman in front of me was wearing a top that said 'United Against Dementia' At first I laughed, envisaging the "UAD" advancing towards a pack of loons in their 80s, all walking around aimlessly, you know and pleasantly confused hollering 'I want to go home.' ……….. Then the tears fell and there was another wave…..I don't feel the waves when I'm with clients though, even the ones whose stories resonate with my own…….They hide quietly in the back room of my mind……..

SCENE 5: "THE CLOAK OF SHAME"

The therapist is in 'consult' with client 1

Client 1: It's hiding…….the tinnitus…….. Thank God. That's the unpredictable thing about tinnitus. You never know when it's going to appear. It's like some kind of audible bully in the playground.

Therapist: Staying with that metaphor of the 'bully in the playground,' when do you feel like that?

Client 1: Always before I go to bed. The minute I do the dishes after dinner, I can feel the anxiety rise and then the tinnitus gets louder. I fear I won't be able to sleep…..

Therapist: …and what's the fear if you don't sleep?

Client 1: That I won't be alert enough for work the next day…..

Therapist: And the fear of not being alert enough……?

Client 1: Then I won't be able to perform to the best of my ability and then I suppose ultimately, I'll lose my job….

Therapist: You mentioned before that you are financially very secure and that money is not an issue, so I'm wondering what the fear about losing your job is?

Client 1: I don't know…it's how I'll be judged by other people…..it's the notion of failing, being kicked out of something, being the one who did something wrong….

Therapist: Like the cloak of shame you just mentioned when you were at your father's grave?

Client 1: Yes, I suppose it is like that. Hadn't put those two together…..

Therapist: Stay with that for a moment. How is your tinnitus?

Client 1: I can hear it now quite loudly. It started up again when I was thinking about being judged if I lost my job.

Therapist: Who would judge you the most?

Client 1: Me…..I suppose…….I'm so accustomed to being in the wrong that if someone bumps into me…I'll apologize and think well there must have been something I was doing that led that person to bump into me. And when it comes to my children, well, I feel so guilty for what I have done to them…..

Therapist: Say a bit more

Client 1: Did I tell you I have an eight-year-old daughter who has also started to hear tinnitus….. In her left ear? This is just the icing on the cake. Ever since she was born there have been issues. When she was born, she couldn't feed properly and had to be fed through her stomach. But there was no logical reason for it. The pregnancy was fine….Even the doctors couldn't understand why it was happening,….granted I was very anxious at times but nothing out of the ordinary. She's always had issues with food. She won't eat at the table with me and my husband. She doesn't like anyone watching her when she eats. But in school, she's fine and eats in the lunch hall with all the other children…….

Just before that day in the graveyard, I noticed she was a little bit dazed, she had that forty-yard stare and I had to call her name a few times to get her attention. I thought she was just tired but then she stopped communicating. She would just start shaking out of the blue and be staring into space. So, I took her to the GP on the morning of the day I went to the graveyard……. and he was diagnosed with tinnitus. Can you believe it? She told him she could hear sounds like rice crispies in her ear………Well that day was a game changer. I don't know how to explain it……..Time and space seemed to collapse and I felt like my eight-year-old self. It freaked me out completely……when we got home from the GP,

I felt that strong invisible force take over……..My husband was working from home that day. I called up the stairs and said I had to go somewhere. That's what I said 'somewhere.' I got into the car and drove to the graveyard. I got out and the next thing I know I'm standing above it. That's when I heard the tinnitus. Then I started to feel a bit detached like I was having a dream while awake…if that makes any sense………

Therapist: Yes that makes sense.

Client 1: Then I remembered that this wasn't the first time I'd heard weird sensations in my ear. It was familiar………. I was the only one that didn't cry the day of my father's funeral. I was really happy, not because I was glad he was dead, of course not, he was the center of my life. It was because………oh God I'm really scared of saying this out loud…….. He wasn't dead to me…….. I've never said that out loud before.

Therapist: How is your tinnitus now?

Client 1: I can't hear it…….

SCENE 6: "I LIED"

The therapist is in 'consult' with client 2

Therapist: It's difficult for you to hear that?

Client 2: Oh behave! (*Laughing*) Look I'm ex-army……..

Therapist: And that means?……..

Client 2: So where were you last week?

Therapist: I apologize again for having to cancel the session at late notice…….it was a situation outside of my control……….

Client 2: Nah nah, that's fine. I wasn't looking for an apology. I was just checking you were ok?…………

Therapist: I'm just thinking out loud……..It's interesting how anytime we get to your feelings you deflect the focus back to me. What do you make of that?………. It seems difficult for you to hear that you can be vulnerable.

Client 2: How is being vulnerable going to help me or get rid of this fucking noise?

Therapist: In my experience with tinnitus clients, tinnitus emerges and causes the most disturbance to those who have been emotionally triggered in the past by anxiety, feeling trapped, feeling isolated, feeling extremely vulnerable. Most significantly, in all these cases they were unable to ask for or receive the help they needed at the time. Emotions that have been unexpressed fester within us like a seeping wound….. The body and the psyche always want to expel what no longer serves us. We are more accepting of the body's natural tendency to expel unwanted toxins, but we are less tolerant of the psyche's need to purge. That's what looking after our mental health can entail…….de-toxifying painful unexpressed emotions. For some reason, our world has judged physical vulnerability as acceptable and mental vulnerability as shameful. Tinnitus can be an inner alarm clock to listen to what is no longer healthy, whether that be habits, belief systems, relationships, etc.

Client 2: ……I told my wife I didn't care………..and that I didn't love her either anymore. I lied. That's when I heard the tinnitus again. Like a pneumatic drill driving through my left ear

Therapist: So when you lied about how you felt about your wife, you perceived tinnitus………..

Client 2: Yeah……..I felt angry and upset.

Therapist: How is your tinnitus now?

Client 2: It's the same!……a bit quieter…….I suppose……..

Therapist: When you are open about how you feel, like when you said just now how you felt angry and upset, your tinnitus is a bit quieter……..

Client 2: Fuck me…..you get paid to just repeat what I've said………I'm in the wrong fucking job………..

Therapist: Sorry……I didn't mean to……

Client 2: No I'm sorry……this is just so difficult and not in my comfort zone at all……….. When I first met my wife, I was messed up in the head, some kind of PTSD, I suppose. I had just got back from a tour of Iraq and then a good friend of mine was murdered…….in broad daylight……*(getting agitated)*…… so how do I get to sleep at night? This keeps me awake……

Therapist: What's happening to you now that made you stand up?

Client 2: Christ can you just be a normal person? Sorry…..and before you ask normal is someone who reacts, who isn't so distant…..oh I don't know what I'm talking about….. How much time do we have left? I'm only doing these sessions because the military is paying for them…….

Therapist: Of course. Because to come to therapy of your own accord would mean you are vulnerable or weak?.......that's just an observation not a criticism…..and I also hear that I appear detached……..I ask you to share your feelings and I don't share anything about myself. It can feel very exposing.…... We have five minutes left.

Client 2: Soon after meeting Lisa, my wife, I lost the plot. My tour of Iraq, injuring my back, and then being discharged without any notice…..was just too much. I was suddenly dumped by everything I knew, everything I had worked hard for….I was in the army since I was 16. It was all I knew and then suddenly I wasn't needed anymore, I wasn't useful. I didn't have a clue who I was when I left. I had no qualifications. I did my GCSEs when I was 20……And then my mate got murdered……Anyway, someone must have called Lisa. She found me completely pissed out of my head, walking through traffic shouting randomly at cars and who knows what else. I'd been on a mad bender for a couple of days, I think. She pulled up alongside me in the car and said 'get the fuck inside.' And we drove for…must have been a few hours… we stayed in a hotel and I told her everything, all about my emotional feelings and stuff and well…….she saved my life……Will you be here next week?

SCENE 7: "I LOVE YOU THE MOST"

Therapist: I won't be here next week……. I managed to get on a flight that leaves this evening. I've had to cancel some sessions. I hate doing that. I've only ever cancelled two sessions in the past four years…...both in the past two weeks…….I was reminded of him…….one of my clients……same background…… the same attitude……..well I realized I wasn't over it and couldn't face the next session…………

Someone has put an offer in on the house and I have to go back home and sign the paperwork and well….. Clear out the house. It catches me in the center of my chest…..when I think about facing it all. My mum finally arrived at her 'final destination' nursing home. When I heard the news, it was as if I'd heard she'd died. A surreal foreboding sense of loss engulfed me. It was the same sensation I got when I suspected that something was initially wrong with her…….. She was over visiting me from Dublin and she was doing some make-up shopping in a local department store and well I was sitting outside because I had the dog with me……….and she came out in floods of tears and said she couldn't remember her pin number when she was paying by card…….I know she suspected it too….I just brushed it off and told her I constantly forget mine too and that it would come back to her when she was more relaxed. I remember feeling so trapped….well it was that same sick to your stomach feeling…when she was finally admitted. I felt I was suffocating with the news and I sensed heavy energy all around my left ear. Well, you can imagine where my thoughts went……..

The only respite from the feeling was being outdoors…... I could breathe there. You know it must be so hard for our souls to be trapped in these bodies……. Sleep brings some comfort, where I can escape……. I'm scared……….. I'm frightened of going back home alone and doing it all by myself. It will be like dismantling a stage set, a place where there was once life, a familiar narrative, then it will become just another blank shell waiting for the next story…….. My biggest fear is that I will be overwhelmed by all the memories and that I will exhume ghosts from the past……and if I meet ghosts, I'll be completely consumed by them and lose myself, go crazy…..well I wouldn't be the only one then!…….. There, another heart palpitation and I've no one to blame this time. Maybe that's my biggest fear…….I'll start to experience what she went through before she was taken to hospital. She kept saying relentlessly for the six weeks prior, 'this isn't my home. I don't like it here. I want to go home.' The difference for me is that it is my home………..and yet it's not, or won't be, very soon…….My parents moved into that house four days before I was born. There are pictures of the three of us with very little furniture…….that's the fear of being trapped in my distorted version of reality.

My father died in that house too. After he passed away there was just me and her. You know I left home 18 years ago almost to the month. So, I'm used to transition and change but this feels more finite, some say life is eternal and nothing ends, it just changes form…….. I'm not quite feeling that at the moment………I know I'm being 'invited to fully engage in what therapy is all about, making peace with the past to look to the future through a clearer lens.' However, this feels less of an invitation and more of a hostage………. I called my mum this morning to see how she was settling into the nursing home and she said 'I'm just about to leave Howth now and head home and I'm going to drive back to Clanbrassil Street because I'm very capable of driving you to know. Your father won't be home till later, so I'll see you back there.' She lived in Howth and grew up in Clanbrassil Street in Dublin. So, she's been drawn back to her home too. Maybe somewhere along the space-time continuum, we'll meet again on the journey 'home.'……….. I woke up during the night after dreaming of being at a party that she was hosting and I recalled the numerous times over the past year, since her diagnosis, that she thanked me for everything……..I am grateful for that. When she has moments of clarity now, she tells me that she loves me and says how we'll go to the theatre again sometime and how she looks forward to coming over to visit me in London……

The last time I saw her, it was the morning I was leaving to come back to London and I wanted her advice, but I knew I had to ask for it differently…… I asked her who she had loved in her life, and that it couldn't be me. I wanted to ask her who she had been in love with the most. I even said it didn't matter if it wasn't my father, I just wanted to know. I wanted to know if it was ok to love…..ok to love…… more than one person……..she said 'I suppose your dad and'…..then it was as if she couldn't process what I had asked her.

Around an hour later I was on the airport hopper bus and she called me and said,' I've been thinking about what you asked, and it's you. I love you the most.' We both cried over the phone. Little did we know the world was going to change irreparably within a few weeks. You know the years of dealing with her anxiety and depression and the frustration of it all …..I think that's why I left home in the first place….to escape her mental ill-health and then I end up being a therapist (laughs)…….but you can't ever really escape anything until you face it squarely……

I miss him and I want to see him again, despite what happened......I know it wasn't professional but you can't always help who you fall in love with.........My biggest fear is that I'll never be loved as much by anyone again.

SCENE 8: "YOU JUST SHARED THE TRUTH"

The therapist is in 'consult' with client 1

Client 1: I was never loved in the same way again. I mean people said, 'I love you.' But the light was gone out in their eyes. There was a palpable barrier. My mother was in the hospital for three months and eventually, she recovered, but the love never did. My sisters never forgave me. I wasn't making it up……do you believe me?

Therapist: I do believe you. But me believing in you does not matter. It's what you believe, that's the most important.

Client 1: Have you ever heard……..tinnitus?

Therapist: What makes you ask?……….do you question how I can help you if I haven't had the same experience as you?……..and that's ok.

Client 1: I just feel so isolated and alone. Like I'm the only one……..

Therapist: None of us are immune to life's challenges and we are all vulnerable…… There are some objects on the table beside you. It can sometimes help to see how we feel from a distance. Can you choose two objects; one to represent the tinnitus and one to represent the feeling of isolation.

Client 1: oh ok……eh I don't know why I'm choosing this one…..but……is this Mufasa from the Lion King?

Therapist: Yes

Client 1: Ok this is me feeling alone and isolated. And then for my tinnitus………eh……….this little skeleton…….

Therapist: What do you notice about where you have placed them?

Client 1: The skeleton is behind the lion. The lion can't see him but he knows he's there…….. (Pauses suddenly)

Therapist: What's happening to you now?

Client 1: I was the only one who heard him, my father ….after he died. It started with feeling a presence or energy, like when you just know someone has walked into the room, without physically seeing or hearing anything. These sensations started the moment he died. I remember I was trying to sleep in the backroom when I heard a commotion and whispering next door. I got up and hung around at the threshold of the room. And I could hear confirmation that he was gone. I heard my aunt saying, 'he's gone, call his sister.' We'll need pennies for his eyes. I've got some in my bag downstairs. I'll go get them.' I suddenly realized that the crackling breathing had silenced. It was a noise that reminded me of crunching leaves……..That was the sound of his breathing that started the day before he died. As I stood there in the doorway I felt a warmth, like a breeze with more substance though, slowly pass across and….. Through me, I suppose. It's all a bit of a blur but I remember the heavy pressure feeling around my left ear. It made the left side of my face feel a bit numb. Then, I started to hear something that resembled a choir or a chanting sound but more primitive. Then it transformed into some kind of white noise……and then ……well…….This all happened within a few days before the funeral.

Therapist: It's difficult to voice exactly what you heard……….how is your tinnitus now?

Client 1: Loud

Therapist: If it could speak what would it say?

Client 1: It would say……..by telling the truth you caused more pain and it was all your fault. That's what I hear most of the time in my head……….a bit like Mufasa here.

Poor Mufasa…..no one understood where his pain came from and why he behaved the way he did.

Therapist: What about in your heart? What does it say? What would Mufasa's heart say?

Client 1: It would say…..you were only eight and you did nothing wrong…..you just shared the truth, you passed on the message…….. (*Takes a big in-breath and sighs it out*). He sounded just like he did when he was alive….except a bit further away…..like when you used to call Australia or somewhere and the person on the other end would sound faint and you'd have to focus to hear everything…… That's what he sounded like. I kept hearing the words 'Robin, robin, robins.' My parents had a joint fascination and respect for robins…….. So, while they were all mourning and planning the funeral, I was feeling very upbeat, having a nice time hearing him around me and it must have shown on my face…because they looked at me as if I was being disrespectful or indifferent……..'But he's ok,' I wanted to shout, but I knew not to. He said things like 'I'm ok.' 'Everything works out just fine,' 'you are never alone.' That gave me so much comfort. I believed him.

Then……on the morning of the funeral……. when we were at the graveside, I looked across the grave…….it was really cold….I was shivering……. and a robin suddenly caught my eye and it was looking straight at me and I must have forgotten myself for a moment because I blurted out, 'There's Dad, he's ok.' My mother asked me who I was talking to, I couldn't keep it in any longer. I said, 'it's Dad, he's not dead, he talks to me.' She collapsed with the shock and probably the mixture of that and the cold. She hit her head on the pavement and lost consciousness. Then she was taken to hospital ……. I think I've blamed myself all these years even though she made a full recovery.

Therapist: If your eight-year-old daughter said something similar to you, about hearing voices, would you chastise and blame her?

Client 1: Of course not! She's only eight, she's only a child…..like I was…….. (*Cries*).

Therapist: If you could advise your eight-year-old self, what would it be?

Client 1: I would tell her it wasn't her fault and to keep looking out for robins…..

SCENE 9: "I FELT EMBARRASSED BY …… A ROBIN"

The therapist is in 'consult' with client 2

Client 2:…….It was a…….. Oh my God…….you won't believe this…….it was a robin….. banging on the bedroom window (*laughs*) and the first thought I had was of you…..that is crazy shit…..(*laughs*)

Therapist: Synchronicities can feel crazy. How did that make you feel……my suggestion just then to notice things in nature like 'robins' and then your account of what happened this morning when you woke up to a robin banging on the window?

Client 2: It's all a bit weird. I don't read much into any of that stuff…..you like all that kind of stuff?

Therapist: Synchronicities can affirm that we are exactly where we should be, reassuring us that we are on the right track. They can provide some comfort in times of distress.

Client 2: Yeah…..Anyway, I started writing down some of my feeling emotions, and……it wasn't easy……….but I felt a bit less angry. I brought them with me. Do you want to see them?

Therapist: Do you want to share them with me?

Client 2: Okay…….(*starts to read from a crumpled up piece of paper*) 'so trapped, can't escape, can't escape this screaming in my ear, not coping with this, the world is crumbling, feel sick, it's all my fault'…..there (*hands paper to therapist*)…..I can't read anymore.

Therapist: What's happening to you now? How are you feeling in your body?

Client 2: My chest….. Around here is…….. (*Hesitantly*) heavy? I don't know about these feelings… emotion…. stuff. Oh, Christ why can't I do this? I'm ex-army for fuck's sake! Sorry I need to stop swearing in front of you. You probably think I'm really weak and pathetic…..I mean you get paid to be nice, right?...... I wish my wife was like you……sorry.

Therapist: You don't like yourself, do you? Why is that?

Client 2: What' you talking about? Nah, nah, don't start that manipulating stuff….

Therapist: I notice that you reject any gesture of kindness and when you feel you've exposed a part of the true you, you push me away. You make assumptions about how I may or may not feel about what you've said or done. These assumptions are not based on the present, they are based on previous experiences with others, and that's ok. That's what we all do. That's how we learn about ourselves and how to be in the world, we learn through our relationships with others. Sometimes the learning is great when we feel loved and cared for and other times it's not, especially when we start to believe the negative stuff that others have said about or to us. What others say does not define who we are, unless we buy into the projection and start to believe in it ourselves. That is one of the most common things I hear from tinnitus clients, they believe they are a limited, distorted version of themselves, a version which belongs to someone else, making them feel unworthy, undeserving and eventually it triggers corrosive self-loathing.

Client 2: Christ, who's the one having therapy here?...... (Both laugh)......If I hadn't seen that fucking robin this morning, I wouldn't have come to this session. I didn't want to come today. But when that fucking bird started tapping on my window.......it was like a reminder from you...it was as if you'd heard my thoughts.....and I felt.....embarrassed that you'd heard me. Christ's sake I felt embarrassed by.... a robin. Maybe I need to see a psychiatrist again......

Therapist: So let's stay with that image of the Robin, knocking on your window. I'm curious to know more about this internal 'conversation,' you had with the Robin. If it were a script or a dialogue between two characters, how would it go? You are asleep, you awaken to the sound of knocking. Who speaks first?

Client 2: I don't know! Eh…….this is silly…….probably the Robin…..saying 'You've got to get up,'

Therapist: Then you respond….

Client 2: Eh,

Therapist: I notice you are smiling

Client 2: Eh yeah, I eh just was remembering something…..I was 21 when I did that tour in Northern Ireland and eh I met a girl…..she liked me and I liked her… We wanted to go out but…at first, she said it was too dangerous….because of where I was from and because of where she was from……I don't know why I'm telling you this……it was the Robin, she cared, she told me 'I had to get up,' one morning after we were together. She didn't want me to get in trouble. No one had done that for me since I was around eight…..(laughs nervously) She didn't judge me either……and she would have had every right to have judged me…..but she didn't. She had the most incredible eyes. She saw me….like she didn't see the uniform at all. It didn't matter. She saw something else, I'll never forget the way she made me feel…..that probably sounds weird……I've never felt that way since…….

Therapist: Is that because you don't feel you deserve to feel that way again? Sorry, go on…

Client 2: We were all getting so sick of the same shit every day….men, women, and children throwing shit at you…..literally…….God, I hated them. I mean I tried to like them, I tried to understand why they did what they did…..but there's only so much you can take….My Sarge used to say, 'we are not here to make enemies or friends, just get on with the job and it's not personal.' And for a few months that was fine, once I eh put my uniform on…that was that…I was doing a job……….So this girl….the one with the eyes….. Well eh, we started seeing each other…..in secret. Christ, if her family had found out her bloke was a British soldier………So fucking dangerous, I could have got us both killed……I didn't know it at the time but I must have eh……loved her because I used to get so nervous going to meet her…….I knew it was wrong but I eh couldn't help myself. Neither could she by the way…………….. I could make her blush easily………. she was …eh I don't know………well to me……..she was like……..she was like a star….something that shone brightly in a very dark place. I used to say to her 'how can someone like you come from a shithole like this?' She'd no idea how beautiful she was ……..I don't think anyone had ever told her…..she was going through a really tough time when I met her…..her dad was in prison and her mother was ill……..she, eh her mother had that eh two polar disorder……I don't think I've got that right…but you know what I mean?…..it meant she had to be a carer for her mother. Her mother would leave the house at night and wander around when she was having some sort of mental episode. That's how I met her actually…..we were on patrol one night and we met this old dear in her dressing gown around 1a.m……..completely lost…….kept saying she was trying to find her home……..she was only around 50 years of age but you would have thought she had dementia or something……..she had her handbag with her address in it so we're able to identify her and bring her home……how mental? Walked out with her dressing gown and a handbag!……….. I don't blame her. If I lived there, I'd have gone fucking mad too…….and well that's when we both first met when we brought her mother home……She was nice, friendly and kept thanking us for helping her mum……..We were not used to that kind of treatment…….'It was nice meeting ya,' she said, in an accent, I was taught to not trust……….(*becomes a bit emotional and fights back tears*) I admired her for what she was doing for her mother. No siblings around to help her or anything…….I'd never met anyone so caring………at least not in my family (*laughs*)………I wanted to be with her forever……you know when you know…….but what did I know at 21? I even told her that……yeah bet you're (*directed towards therapist*) shocked to hear that…….see I used to have feeling emotions….. (*Laughs*)

I'd say we saw each other around seven more times and one evening I was on my way to meet her……………when one of our Saracens pulled over…….and my Sarge jumped out and said 'get in.' They had found out what I was doing and ……..where I was going…………I was brought back to the barracks and discharged the next morning back to the UK. They said if I tried to contact her again, I'd be discharged from the army for good………..so that was that………I felt so sick and trapped on the way back to the barracks…….I thought I was going to go mad…….knowing that she'd be waiting……..and thinking that I'd abandoned her…….but sick at the thought that the one bit of joy I had in my life was gone forever……..She told me once how she had thought about killing herself when the old man went down for paramilitary activity…….not because she couldn't cope with her mother or anything…..but because she thought she was the cause of her parents' problems and that maybe their problems would magically disappear if she wasn't around. Her mother had that baby sad disorder……you know when you've had kids……and she thought she was to blame. Her mother had had something like eleven miscarriages before she was born…..so she was probably a bit fucked up from that………She said after we'd met, that I'd reminded her of why she was still alive and that it was because we were meant to meet……..she was such a romantic……omg……..(*remembering fondly*) always saying stuff like we were meant to meet to teach the world that love is love and that religion and where you're from doesn't matter………she said we had a life mission together to teach people that it was ok to love…………she was into all that weird shit…..a bit like you (*laughs*)………..so of course my first thoughts were ……that if she did kill herself, it would be because of what I did……..I know it wasn't my fault leaving her……It was the guilt I felt afterwards. If I had just left her alone, then I wouldn't have given her hope………that's worse I think…….losing something amazing than never having it at all.

Therapist: Is that how *you* felt afterwards?

Client 2: I thought my heart was never gonna get fixed…….

Therapist: How is your tinnitus now? How are you feeling?

Client 2: Eh......... I can't hear it..........ah, there it is.......bit quieter. How do I feel? Shit.........Nah nah not in that way....sorry.......I feel drained.......I won't ever be able to forget what I did but....... I probably deserved it though.......phew.......God, didn't expect to get this off my chest

Therapist: How does holding onto the guilt benefit your life now?

Client 2: What?

Therapist: Would you like to enjoy your life more? Or would you prefer to feel guilt for something that was not your fault? Both of you were adults and you both decided to be together. In the same way, we all have a decision to take our own lives or not. It's a choice...... I often get told by clients that 'killing themselves will relieve their tinnitus.' 'How can you be sure of that?' I ask them. 'It could be ten times worse.' At least by choosing to live we can work on ways of managing it and potentially finding the root cause of a lot of misery and unhappiness that trigger the tinnitus.... In my experience clients often gain even more joy and quality of life, as a result of identifying and letting go of the rotting toxic obstacles, such as guilt, that stop them from engaging in life as fully as possible. If that girl were here now and heard our conversation, what do you think she would say….without censoring….go with what comes to mind first.

Client 2: Eh,……….. She'd say don't worry about it, that's what I thought happened that day….something like that….maybe……. I've never thought that she might say something like that……..ok…….yeah……..I don't know…….it still doesn't take away the physical sensation of tinnitus……………..

Therapist: Tinnitus, like most crises, happens for a reason……it's not easy to hear that, I know.

Client 2: Explain that one……sorry you've lost me.

Therapist: It…….or should I say any upset/episode…..call it what you will…..asks us to listen to the noise within, to recognize some blind spot about the true nature of ourselves….our circumstances, that has been previously concealed…..

Reflections on *The Noise Within*

Therapy Process

"Life can only be understood backwards, but it must be lived forwards."

Soren Kierkegaard.

The rationale for The Noise Within

My intention for *The Noise Within* is to educate and provide vicarious support to tinnitus sufferers and anyone who feels stuck in cycles of anxiety and despair. We all experience physical, emotional, and spiritual crises at different times in our lives. It can trigger feelings of apathy, loss, depression, anxiety, and despair, rendering the road ahead unimaginable. We are often left feeling helpless and consequently struggle to find meaning in our world. I use the term 'we' because we are all aboard this human journey! Therapists like myself are no different.

By taking the courageous step to engage in any kind of therapy, coaching, healing, and creative self-reflection we can empower ourselves to dare to live a more fulfilling and purposeful life than the one before, a life that is more aligned with our true selves. The crisis, although in some cases life-changing, is often a blessing in disguise as it serves as a catalyst to unlocking the previously unknown potential within ourselves and hence guides us to make positive changes, for a better future. Like the symbol of the phoenix, renewal, and rebirth follow struggle, crisis, and change.

I hope the content of *The Noise Within* will also encourage therapists to become interested and confident in providing emotional support for tinnitus clients.

What is Tinnitus?

Tinnitus is the involuntary perception of sound within the ear of the head. The nature of the sounds perceived is variable (i.e. hissing, ringing, shushing, buzzing, etc.) but the majority of cases would report perceiving a high-pitched signal.

Tinnitus Treatments

It is important to note that there are a variety of methods that are used globally to treat the symptom of tinnitus. These include the application of sound-based therapies, hearing aids, neuromodulation techniques, physiotherapy, and transcranial magnetic stimulation protocols. At the time of writing, this is not a dedicated pharmaceutical therapy for subjective tinnitus perception. I have drawn knowledge from the numerous experts in the field of tinnitus. I work collaboratively with ENT and Audiological specialists to provide a holistic healthcare package for clients, using a combination of treatment approaches, namely *Tinnitus Desensitization Therapy*, with my Integrative Therapy Model. The combination of audiological and psychological elements has proven to be very successful. However, the majority of my clients are referred to me because they are in the early stage of tinnitus or they are not suitable for audiological treatments. For that reason, I am focusing purely on the psychological aspect of support in *The Noise Within*.

Tinnitus and Mental Health

Tinnitus is a condition that is heavily influenced by emotional states. Some people's experience of tinnitus makes them feel stressed, tense, anxious, and depressed. These feelings are not always instigated by tinnitus, but they can be exacerbated by it. It is well known that tinnitus can become very problematic when the experience of tinnitus itself induces anxiety. It is also well documented how an increase in emotional reactions can exacerbate the volume, pitch, and sound of the tinnitus perception. When this happens, a vicious cycle ensues as stress renders tinnitus worse, which, subsequently, leads to greater stress and anxiety.

I hope *The Noise Within* will encourage those experiencing bothersome tinnitus to seek emotional and psychological support to reduce the emotional impact of their tinnitus as well as becoming curious about what it signifies to them. My aim in this series of play-scripts and guidebooks is manifold.

To expose how psychological therapy in the majority of cases is the most appropriate means of reducing tinnitus distress and leading to habituation.

One of the first questions that clients ask me is '*Will I be stuck with this sound forever?*' Similar to Client 1 and Client 2 in the play, they are extremely anxious and have reached a crisis point. They both feel trapped. Client 1, in particular, demonstrates her despair at tinnitus by contemplating suicide. We understand from her story that she has undergone some trauma in her early life, which has greatly impacted her self-limiting beliefs. These self-limiting beliefs about '*doing something wrong*' haunt her throughout her life. Tinnitus occurs when a memory from childhood is triggered. The memory includes the death of a parent and their subsequent funeral, where she was punished for sharing her experience of hearing her father after he passed away. This is the root of her trauma, where she appears to be emotionally stuck because the outcome of her revelation had painful consequences. But this was not her fault, she was a child who was grieving for her father.

Client 2 has experienced several incidents of trauma that unfold throughout his sessions. The most pertinent one is the guilt he feels over the girl he left. He becomes emotionally trapped thereafter. His tinnitus is triggered after that event and again more recently in a similar relational dynamic, where he has ignored how he feels and is not able to express his truth, not to mention the traumas he encountered previously in the armed forces. It could be argued that his tinnitus was triggered by noise exposure. This is no doubt a strong contributor to his condition. However, he is emotionally incited and influenced by his tinnitus. This demonstrates how Client 1 requires psychological support to understand and regulate his emotions, to reduce his tinnitus perception. Research (Hinton et al 2006) indicates that PTSD is another precursor of bothersome tinnitus perception.

These experiences of trauma are very common in my experience as a therapist working with tinnitus clients. If the trauma has not been adequately processed near the time it occurs, clients often remain in a state of fight or flight, which Van der Kolk (2014) highlights, increases their sensitivity to threatening noises. This explains why tinnitus can be very traumatizing from its onset because it is activating a prior trauma, which holds the same emotional distress as tinnitus. This, of course, is only apparent in cases that I meet in my therapy practice. Not everyone who experiences tinnitus suffers emotionally from it and is, therefore, more suited to an audiological treatment approach.

This heightened state of fight or flight awakens the older limbic brain and allows it to take over, which creates more tension and anxiety in the body. The limbic system is the part of the brain involved in our emotional and behavioral responses, especially those associated with fear and panic; fight or flight. This greatly impacts the throat, middle ear, and voice box, which is why tension and anxiety exacerbate tinnitus perception. If we continue to remain in this state, the body eventually becomes so overwhelmed that it enters the 'emergency' state and shuts down through collapse or fainting. Some of my clients often claim how they had a 'breakdown' at the initial onset of their tinnitus; they couldn't go to work, couldn't get out of bed, etc.

In Client 1's case, her original trauma emerged after she 'voiced' something, Therefore, her trauma remained wedged in the throat/middle ear/voice box area of the body. It is plausible to consider that her trauma was later expressed as tinnitus. So, therefore, it could be argued that her 'emergency' state was expressed through her suicidal ideation. She could no longer sustain her levels of anxiety and wanted to escape it. Luckily, she eventually reached out and asked for help. Van der Kolk and Levine, to name but a few, have widely documented the link between an overactive limbic system, owing to trauma and physical and mental ill-health. The reverse is also true; the more regulated we become through mental and emotional wellbeing, the healthier our physical state becomes.

So how does therapy reduce anxiety and trauma states? Social engagement/interaction is a key ingredient in the reduction of fight or flight states of being. Being seen and understood by another human helps clients to learn how to self-regulate and how to calm down. It also reduces tinnitus perception.

'Being able to feel safe with other people is probably the single most important aspect of mental health, safe connections are fundamental to meaningful and satisfying lives.'

(Van der Kolk)

Additionally, social engagement through therapy enables clients to unpack (in some cases unconscious) self-limiting belief patterns, that keep the trauma alive in the present, and to recognize how belief systems influence the client's state of anxiety. Identifying and disentangling these beliefs is at the core of my therapeutic approach. In the play, Client 1 needed to identify where her belief about '*always doing something wrong*' originated. This was a hard-wired belief, instigated during a traumatic event in her early life, which became re-triggered when she encountered similar dynamics. She found it easier to engage with her feelings with the therapist unlike Client 2. Client 2's feelings of guilt and suppressed anger required gentle disentangling and processing. He needed to feel safe and trusting in the sessions to share his '*feeling emotions.*' He initially distances himself from his feelings as if they are something alien to him. Understandably, expressing emotions was not something he was used to doing prior, and this needed time. Emotion is a relational concept and acts as the interface between the internal world of the client and the beliefs and values that influence their external circumstances (Mullen, 2017). If the outer circumstances are not hospitable to expressing emotions, it can generate internal blocks within the client and externally in the therapeutic relationship.

This was apparent for Client 2 initially and impeded any relief in his tinnitus perception. It was only through the development of a relationship with the therapist that he began to trust her and to share his story. This was rocky at the beginning as he expressed a lot of passive aggression towards her. However, the therapy held a non-judgmental and compassionate space for him, which allowed him to begin to trust her and most importantly himself. This was further exemplified by the synchronistic occurrence of the robin that demonstrated a clear shift in Client 2's relationship with the therapist. Carl Jung believed that synchronistic events such as this provide clues as to how we are all connected (Mac Gregor & Mac Gregor, 2010). Serendipitously, it was Jung himself who coined the term synchronicity after he glanced and witnessed an insect tapping at the window while in consult with a client. The client had just told him about a dream, which included this very insect, which Jung perceived immediately after she mentioned the dream. (The story of the robin tapping on the window is a true event that occurred in my therapeutic practice).

When we sense this connection through these types of experiences, we feel less isolated in the world and we open up more to others, and most significantly, we open up to ourselves. For Client 2, this moment was crucial for enabling him to give himself access to his vulnerability and subsequently share the part of him that knew joy and love with the therapist. His tinnitus was less bothersome thereafter. Client 1 is soothed by the sight of robins as she associates this with her father in the afterlife. She feels less separated from him and subsequently less mournful.

Therapeutic techniques such as having a supportive space to acknowledge and process events, investigate self-limiting belief systems, and acquiring an understanding of how to de-regulate anxious states, are integral to habituation and the eventual management of tinnitus perception.

To illuminate the possibility of habituation to tinnitus, through self-exploration and subsequently self-knowledge, that can lead to a happier life than before

'Habituation is a reduction in the emotional relevance of the noise of tinnitus. It enables the filtration of tinnitus from conscious awareness. If you care less you perceive it less'

(Mark Williams, Tinnitus Audiologist & Specialist, Harley St, London).

Once both of the characters in the play recognized some of their fearful cycles of thinking, they noticed a reduction in their tinnitus. They both had to work through their resistance or fear of disappointment, to understand that habituation is possible through self-awareness. The dominant pattern of thinking amongst tinnitus clients, in my experience, is that there is no cure! This is a fundamental obstacle to habituation. Often this is another example of an over-active limbic system, owing to trauma, as previously discussed; it is safer to prepare for the worst. However, I encourage my clients to notice how powerful their fearful thoughts are and how they can immediately diminish their feelings of wellbeing, to highlight the power of thoughts over our feelings in general. If we can allow fearful thoughts to influence how we feel, we can also allow more hopeful thoughts to influence our feelings. This requires, first of all, an understanding of the negative cycle of fearful thoughts, where they originate, and then secondly, deciding to let go of the self-limiting beliefs, formed through repetitive fearful thinking, that no longer serve us. This is a process that requires time, effort, and the willingness to make positive changes, but it pays dividends in the end.

In most of my clinical practice, this is the key ingredient to habituation: self-knowledge and self-awareness. Once this is achieved, it automatically leads to positive changes in beliefs and ultimately positive choices and positive outcomes, resulting in habituation. Most significantly, clients report feeling happier and more empowered in their lives than they did before tinnitus.

The contrary is also true, those who are resistant to identifying the power of fearful thought cycles struggle to make positive changes and consequently fail to notice any changes in their tinnitus. This is by no means a criticism. Everyone is at different stages on their journey and can only acquire self-awareness and make the courageous step to change thinking patterns when they are ready. It cannot be forced. However, I share this here, and in my practice, as I feel it would be a huge dis-service to let clients believe that just showing up at sessions would be suffice to heal. My method is guided by the principle of self-empowerment, providing clients with tools for them to self-regulate, self-flourish and to become sovereign beings, and trust their inner authority in their recovery. The therapist in the play tells the clients '*You are the expert of you.*' Therapists, in my view, are guides and teachers and their role is to unlock the client's inner guide and teacher.

In *The Noise Within*, both clients felt relieved to have shared their stories and were more at peace within themselves. Whilst they still are in the process of therapy in the play, they are both more self-aware and therefore, able to begin to let go of the traumas that were keeping them stuck.

To share insight into the untold world of the therapist, to highlight the universality of suffering and experiencing life crises

There can be a myth that therapists *'have it all sorted'* which can be an obstacle to engaging in therapy for the client. They can fear being exposed and judged. I felt this way too when I first engaged in therapy. In *The Noise Within*, Client 2 claims he only attends the sessions because an organization is paying for it. So, resistance to acquiring help can be hindered by a fear of what therapy may entail; it can feel exposing, especially when it can involve being vulnerable. If therapy is something that jars with our beliefs about what it means to be vulnerable, it can impede us from reaching out for therapeutic support. Therefore, it can feel safer and more containing for some to be 'referred' by an organization. This was integral to Client 2's recovery as he may not otherwise have sought out emotional support independently. In the play, the therapist needed to be having therapy herself as her narrative was triggered by this client and she was processing her life-changing circumstances.

The therapist also reassures Client 1 that *'none of us are immune to life's challenges and we are all vulnerable.'* The therapist's hardship is very much alive at the time she is treating these clients. She is coming to terms with her mother's terminal illness. My message in my practice is to reassure clients and potential clients of the universality of life experience and that they are not alone. Whilst I do not share personal content in therapy sessions with my clients, I do remind them that they are not alone and that I too engage in therapy. This tends to reduce some of their anxiety as the universality of experience is a curative factor, the notion that we are not isolated in our experience of emotional pain. However, as evidenced in the play, it is not always easy to conceal personal indicators such as accent, cultural background, etc. Client 1 makes an assumption about the therapist based on her nationality. Client 2 is triggered by the therapist's accent as it recalled a traumatic event in his life. Being curious about how these obvious factors, related to identity, can form the subtext of our interpersonal dynamics with others, can deepen our understanding and our compassion for both ourselves and our clients and thus generate a multi-layered transformation of belief systems that stretch beyond the 'here and now to include the 'there and then' (Mullen, 2018).

Therefore, it is vital to demystify the notion of the 'untroubled therapist,' described unapologetically by Marie Adams for therapists whose 'backstory' is very often untold, but one that can fortify their empathy and compassion for their clients and deepen their self-knowledge along this path we call life.

Within this realm of 'universality,' all three characters are implicitly and explicitly facing and processing the ultimate universal experience; death. It resides in the backdrop as a destination they are all heading towards. They have all experienced the death of others in their life and for some, they have felt close to It themselves. However, it haunts all three, regardless of whether or not they claim indifference to it. In my clinical experience, the root fear that dwells within all clients who see me for support is a fear of dying. It starts with a fear of tinnitus being with them eternally and extends to a fear of losing control, a fear of not coping, and then a fear of death.

Michael Meade describes how modern societies postpone questions about death until the end, compared to traditional cultures that ritualize death as much as they do birth. The natural cycle of life is respected and becomes an impetus to living life, not merely existing. Meade accurately observes that *'since life includes death, an exaggerated fear of death can only lead to a growing fear of life'* (2012:87). To some extent all three characters in *The Noise Within* portray a fear of 'living' life, it takes physical symptoms, namely, tinnitus and heart palpitations, and the characters' encounter with themselves and each other, through therapy, to awaken them to inadvertently face their mortality and to permit themselves to start to 'live' their lives. Each character encounters the antithesis of death, life, through the symbol of the robin which denotes the natural cycle of life; birth, death, and renewal as well as a reminder to take a risk to believe and to say 'yes' to life and actively take part in it. I believe this to be more relevant now than ever before in our world as I write these words in 2021.

Model of Therapy for Tinnitus

My current integrative model of clinical practice explores the application of Dramatherapy with strategies from Cognitive Behavioural Therapy, and the Humanist Model, with clients experiencing acute anxiety and depression, as a result of a sudden onset of tinnitus perception. Tinnitus does not negatively affect everyone who perceives it. My clients are referred for the very reason that tinnitus is having a severe impact on their mental health and lives in general. This model has evolved out of a therapeutic model originally designed to help reduce despair and anxiety in clients suffering from tinnitus.

As the method has progressed distinctive patterns began to emerge that stretched beyond a relaxation-focused approach to a deeper exploration of the potential roots of the anxiety. This positively influences not just the client's reaction to their tinnitus but equips them with the transferrable tools to manage anxiety in any given circumstance.

The method has also begun to highlight the importance of clients listening to a deeper meaning/calling that is triggered by their tinnitus; the individual's true soul identity and purpose. In numerous cases, clients often lack a sense of meaning or fulfillment in their lives. Some claim how they have never considered what they want from life. They are more preoccupied with looking after others. This potential *'calling'* occurs in times of crisis. Since the client is not yet consciously willing to acknowledge that *'the way things were,'* is obsolete, they are not cognizant that their tinnitus and acute anxiety, is *'signalling that major change is required for successful and evolutionary adaptation'* (Peck 1978:59).

Dramatherapy

Dramatherapy is one of the HCPC regulated psychological disciplines (Health and Care Professions Council) arts therapies that utilize the art form for therapeutic benefit. The medium of art, drama, and creative expression are used to facilitate the communication of feelings indirectly. Talking and thinking are also a vital part of the work. Thomas Khun maintained that you cannot see something unless you have the correct metaphor to enable you to perceive it. Dramatherapy is defined as 'the intentional and systematic use of drama processes to achieve psychological change and growth' (Emunah 1994:3). One of the objectives of Dramatherapy is the relief of suffering through aesthetic distancing. The Dramatherapy concept of 'aesthetic distancing' is utilized as a part of the integrative therapy model, in the treatment of tinnitus clients, to enable them to both access their feelings towards the signal whilst also maintaining an observer stance. The emotions triggered by tinnitus can be very overwhelming and traumatizing for clients which can impede their ability to self-regulate and to observe how their negative thought patterns are entrapping them. The use of imagery and objects in dramatherapy to explore their tinnitus can provide a safe distance for clients due to the images/objects being seen as separate from the self.

This was evident in the play with both Client 1 and Client 2. The use of objects enabled Client 1 to voice the unspoken story about her father which had troubled her for years. It facilitated her to recount the story in a calm and self-regulated way, through aesthetic distancing.

Client 2 brought his image to the session, the robin, which triggered his untold story, the source of his trauma. This acted as a portal to his emotions and feelings that had been suppressed and operated as a gateway to developing trust with the therapist.

Metaphor and aesthetic distancing have been used with PTSD clients to help them modulate and express affect (James & Johnson 1996, Landy 2003). The emotional reactions to tinnitus can be compared to feelings of a lack of control as experienced as a result of trauma with tinnitus potentially being evaluated as harmful, which can induce severe anxiety. The duration of tinnitus is unpredictable, and the client feels a loss of control over the condition (Jun et al 2013). This induces a 'fight or flight' reaction within the client as a result of their emotional reaction developing into a phobic state. Lahad and Doron (2010) promote the collaborative approach of utilizing both creative methods and cognitive behavioral therapy in the treatment of anxiety disorders and P.T.S.D. Dramatherapy techniques utilized include Story-making, Embodiment-Projection- Role, and Ritual Theatre. It offers clients the opportunity to creatively explore the phenomenon of tinnitus and the role it plays as an internal satellite navigational tool to self-knowledge.

Cognitive Behavioural Therapy

Similar to depressive clients, some tinnitus clients have improbable and overt negative thoughts relating to their tinnitus. CBT aims to identify these automatic negative thoughts, gauge their cogency, and substitute them with more realistic and positive thoughts. This procedure is referred to as cognitive restructuring (Jin Jun 2013). Cognitive therapy cannot eliminate tinnitus; however, it is one of the most prolifically utilized and validated methods applied to help individuals with bothersome tinnitus (Martinez-Devesa P. et al 2010). Automatic negative thinking plays a role in inducing and exacerbating the negative emotional reaction to tinnitus. It is ultimately what kept Client 1 and Client 2 stuck in fear and anxiety, thus exacerbating their tinnitus perception. Becoming aware of the negative cycle of thoughts and breaking the pattern is crucial to the reduction of distress and the promotion of habituation. Since Hallam et al (1985) and Sweetow (1986) first introduced CBT for tinnitus in the 1980s, many studies have demonstrated the value of this approach (Jin Jun & Kyun Park 2013).

The Humanist Model

This is based on the Rogerian model of therapy that places clients at the center of the work. Carl Rogers (1995) believed that the fulfillment of personal potential includes sociability, the need to be with other human beings, and a desire to know and be known, by others. It also includes being open to experience, being trusting and trustworthy, being curious about the world, being creative and compassionate. This environment can be achieved when being in a relationship with a deeply, understanding person, i.e. being able to see the client from the client's perspective and communicating that understanding to the client, having unconditional positive regard, being non-judgemental and congruent with the client. This was crucial for the sessions with Client 2. Rogers maintained that these key elements were integral to individuals achieving self-actualization; a person attaining their goals and wishes.

By listening attentively, the practitioner can begin to perceive the difficulties from the client's point of view and begin to help them to see things more clearly, possibly from a different perspective. Acceptance and respect for the client are essentials for a practitioner working with any individual and, as the relationship develops, so too does trust between the practitioner and client. This was vital to creating a rapport with the clients in the play. They only shared what was most painful, when they felt contained and unconditionally regarded by the therapist. This enables the client to look at their condition, attitude, and behavior with respect to their issues and potential treatment pathways. Most importantly, it enables tinnitus sufferers to feel heard and understood regarding an invisible condition that is extremely debilitating and often overlooked by society.

Self-help Exercises

Here are two examples of techniques used to aid relaxation and to gain an overall perspective on the experience of tinnitus so far. During an initial consultation, I facilitate the 'life map exercise. The aim is for the client to observe their experience of tinnitus from an aerial perspective. When appropriate, I invite clients to try different relaxation techniques to see which works for them. Here are examples below.

Creative Techniques

Create a 'timeline or life map that demonstrates when your tinnitus began and identify when it got worse, got better, etc. Add how the tinnitus has impacted your lives/feelings/functionality. Document what was happening in your life in and around the onset of the initial tinnitus and any subsequent period of significant change. The act of looking at the timeline of your tinnitus distances you from the internal dialogue of negative thinking and often highlights significant incidents that you may have forgotten that occurred before the initial onset of their tinnitus. The re-narration of the history of tinnitus enables desensitization by talking about your tinnitus. Does additional exploration include noticing if there are any patterns? What core beliefs influence your current thoughts and feelings? Does a deterioration of your tinnitus coincide with similar events/life changes etc.?

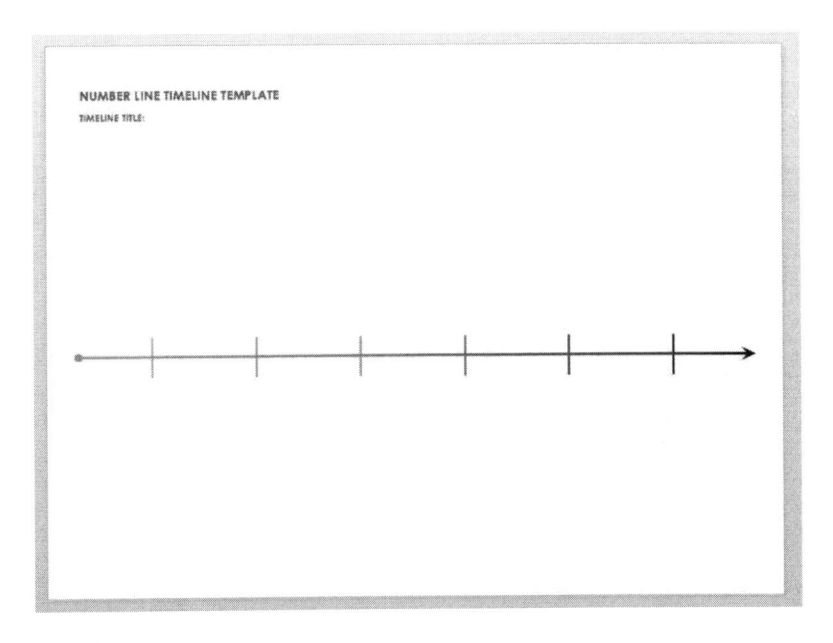

NUMBER LINE TIMELINE TEMPLATE
TIMELINE TITLE:

Relaxation Techniques: Somatic Sensing & Awareness

It is vital to find a balance between fearful and optimistic thought processes. Becoming aware of how our body feels in the here and now can help us identify when we are becoming tense, which, consequently, can exacerbate our perception of tinnitus. Focusing on the present through somatic and body awareness is also crucial for disrupting the negative thought patterns. Practice this relaxation and awareness exercise daily for at least fourteen days.

•Lie on your back, or sit comfortably, legs uncrossed, arms relaxed at your sides, eyes open or closed. Focus on your breathing, allowing your stomach to rise as you inhale and fall as you exhale. Breathe deeply for about two minutes, until you start to feel comfortable and relaxed.

•Turn your focus to the toes of your right foot. Notice any sensations you feel while continuing to also focus on your breathing. Imagine each deep breath flowing to your toes. Remain focused on this area for one to two minutes.

•Move your focus to the sole of your right foot. Tune in to any sensations you feel in that part of your body and imagine each breath flowing from the sole of your foot. After one or two minutes, move your focus to your right ankle and repeat. Move to your calf, knee, thigh, hip, and then repeat the sequence for your left leg. From there,

move up the torso, through the lower back and abdomen, the upper back and chest, and the shoulders. Pay close attention to any area of the body that causes you pain or discomfort.

•Move your focus to the fingers on your right hand and then move up to the wrist, forearm, elbow, upper arm, and shoulder. Repeat for your left arm. Then move through the neck and throat, and finally all the regions of your face, the back of the head, and the top of the head. Pay close attention to your jaw, chin, lips, tongue, nose, cheeks, eyes, forehead, temples, and scalp. When you reach the very top of your head, let your breath reach out beyond your body and imagine yourself hovering above yourself.

•After completing the body scan, relax for a while in silence and stillness, noting how your body feels. Then open your eyes slowly. Take a moment to stretch, if necessary.

References

Adams, M., 2013. The myth of the untroubled therapist: Private life, professional practice. Routledge.

Emunah, R., 1994. Acting for Real: Drama Therapy Process. Technique, and Performance USA, Brunner/Mazel.

Hallam, R.S., Jakes, S.C., Chambers, C., and Hinchcliffe, R., 1985. A comparison of different methods for assessing the 'intensity of tinnitus. *Acta oto-laryngologica*, 99(5-6), pp.501-508.

Hinton, D.E., Chhean, D., Pich, V., Hofmann, S.G. and Barlow, D.H., 2006. Tinnitus among Cambodian refugees: relationship to PTSD severity. *Journal of Traumatic Stress: Official Publication of The International Society for Traumatic Stress Studies*, 19(4), pp.541-546.

James, M. and Johnson, D.R., 1996. Drama therapy for the treatment of affective expression in posttraumatic stress disorder.

Landy, R.J., Luck, B., Conner, E. and McMullian, S., 2003. Role Profiles: a drama therapy assessment instrument. *The arts in psychotherapy*, 30(3), pp.151-161.

Jun, H.J. and Park, M.K., 2013. Cognitive-behavioral therapy for tinnitus: evidence and efficacy. *Korean Journal of audiology*, 17(3), p.101.Jin Jun & Kyun Park 2013

Lahad, M. and Doron, M., 2010. Protocol for treatment of post-traumatic stress disorder: See far cbt model: *Beyond cognitive behavior therapy* (Vol. 70). IOS Press.

Mac Gregor, T. and Mac Gregor, R., 2010. The 7 Secrets of Synchronicity: Your Guide to Finding Meanings in Signs Big and Small. Hay House.

Martinez-Devesa P, Perera R, Theodoulou M, Waddell A. (2010) Cognitive-behavioral therapy for tinnitus. *Cochrane Database Syst Rev (9):CD005233*

Meade, M., 2012. Fate and Destiny: The Two Agreements of the Soul. Green Fire Press.

Mullen-Williams, J., 2017. Strategies from Dramatherapy supervision to augment newly qualified secondary school teachers' experience of self-efficacy and coping strategies in their new role (Doctoral dissertation, Anglia Ruskin University).

Peck, M.S., 1998. The road less travelled and beyond: Spiritual growth in an age of anxiety. Simon and Schuster.

Rogers, C.R., 1995. On becoming a person: A therapist's view of psychotherapy. Houghton Mifflin Harcourt.

Sweetow, R.W., 1986. Cognitive aspects of tinnitus patient management. *Ear and Hearing*, 7(6), pp.390-396.

Van der Kolk, B., 2014. The body keeps the score: Mind, brain, and body in the transformation of trauma. Penguin UK.

About the Author

I am a UK (H.C.P.C) registered Dramatherapist and Badth (British Association of Dramatherapists) registered clinical supervisor. I currently work in education, healthcare, and private practice. Drama and theatre have always played a central role in my life. It encompasses my career in theatre, teaching drama/theatre studies, and practicing as a Dramatherapist. In all areas, I have experienced and witnessed the incredible healing potential of Drama and theatre to facilitate creativity, imagination, learning, insight, change, and growth. I remain actively involved in therapeutic theatre projects. I have also written for the online magazine Your Tango. I lectured at Anglia Ruskin University for seven years (undergraduate Drama programme and MA Dramatherapy programme) and was a visiting lecturer at Central School of Speech and Drama and Roehampton University (UK). I have facilitated students from Mountview in autobiographical theatre. I have been a visiting lecturer at the Han University, Nijmegen (The Netherlands).

My most recent clinical work includes working with children and adolescents and devising theatre-based programmes, underpinned by Dramatherapy, that support literacy, cultivate emotional literacy, self-development, and creativity in both primary and secondary schools (Project Phoenix).

I am a qualified secondary school teacher and I've taught drama for over ten years in secondary and further education. I have also worked collaboratively with professional theatre companies on projects (National Theatre Shell Connections Programme, The Barbican in a Box project with Complicite and the Shakespeare School Festivals) that have proved to raise students' self-esteem and sense of self-efficacy which they can translate to other parts of their lives.

My doctorate research supported the transition of trainee teachers to NQTS. It investigated the efficacy of employing strategies from Dramatherapy supervision with newly qualified teachers as a method of reducing attrition rates Mullen-Williams, Julianne (2018) *Strategies from Dramatherapy supervision to augment newly qualified secondary school teachers' experience of self-efficacy and coping strategies in their new role.* Doctoral thesis, Anglia Ruskin University. https://arro.anglia.ac.uk/703778/

I provide creative supervision and consultation to all helping professionals including therapists, hospice nurses, teachers, medics, social workers, and audiologists. I have designed and facilitated mental health awareness training for the Metropolitan Police and other frontline service staff. I have also co-facilitated retreats (Re-Treat) abroad that focus on Self-Care and reducing burnout amongst professionals https://novareid.com/services/wellbeing-mentoring/retreats/

I currently run reflective practice sessions for teaching staff and courses for parents entitled *Play and Connect* for parents struggling to manage their children's behavior at home.

Qualifications

PhD in Dramatherapy – Anglia Ruskin University, Cambridge

M.A. Dramatherapy – Roehampton University London, HCPC registered, Badth member

Clinical Supervisor – Diploma in Clinical Supervision, TPE

Qualified Teacher Status – Middlesex University

M.A. Drama Studies – University College Dublin

B. Social Science – University College Dublin

Printed in Great Britain
by Amazon